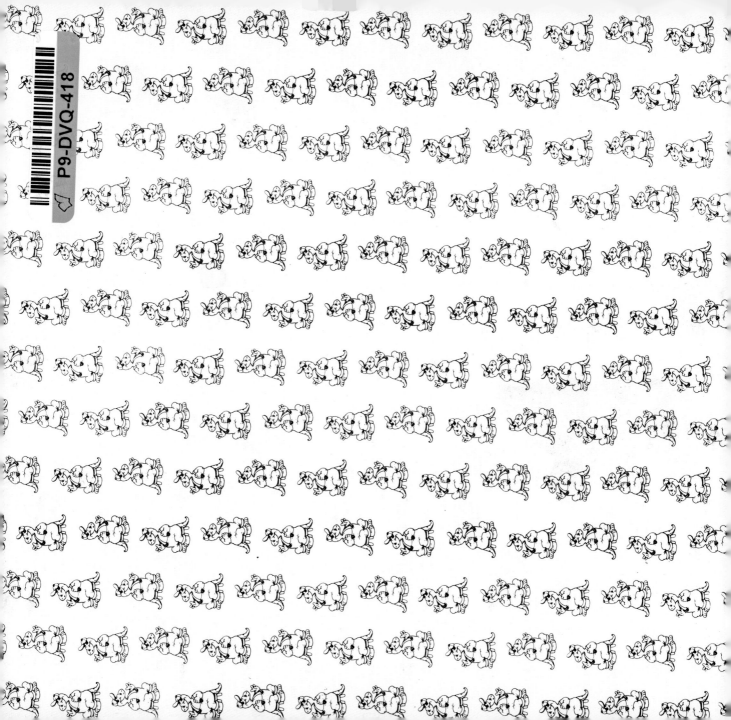

A·FIRST·BOOK·OF COLORS

A·FIRST·BOOK·OF COLORS

Illustrated by David Anstey

Written by A J Wood

MODERN PUBLISHING
A Division of Unisystems, Inc.
New York, New York 10022

One BLUE dinosaur
swam to the shore...

One ORANGE dinosaur
drank juice through a straw.

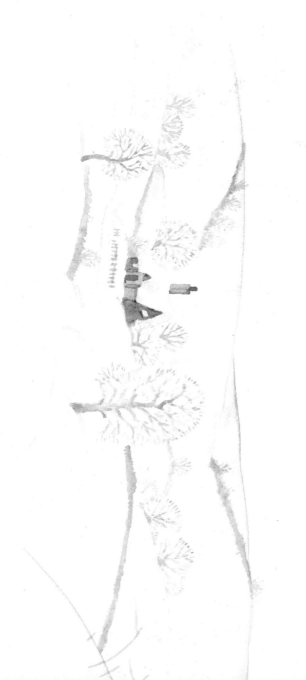

One WHITE dinosaur
played in the snow...

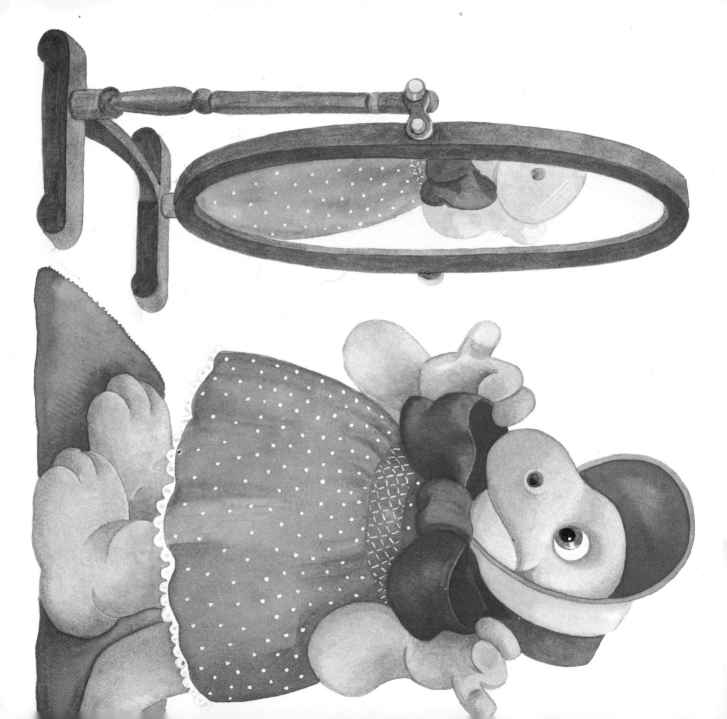

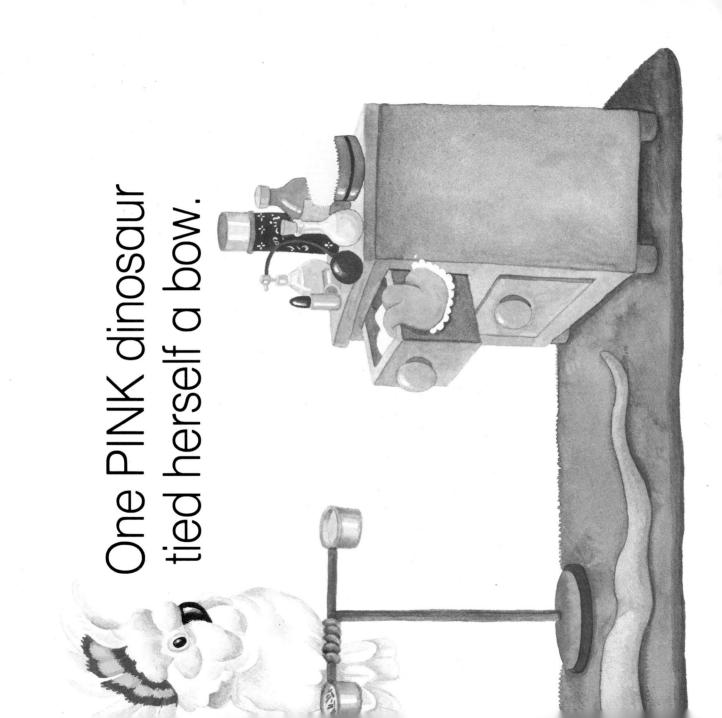

One PINK dinosaur
tied herself a bow.

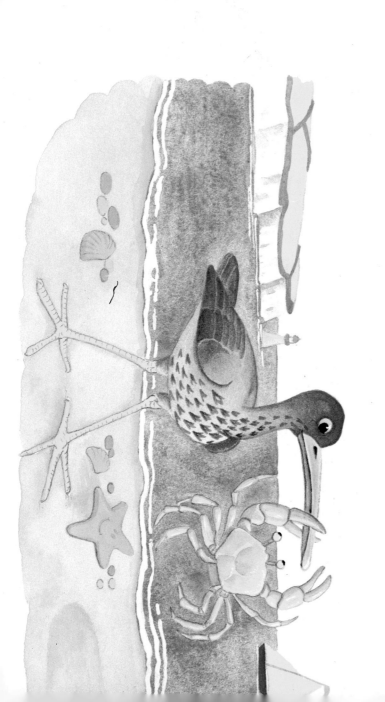

One YELLOW dinosaur went
to the beach...

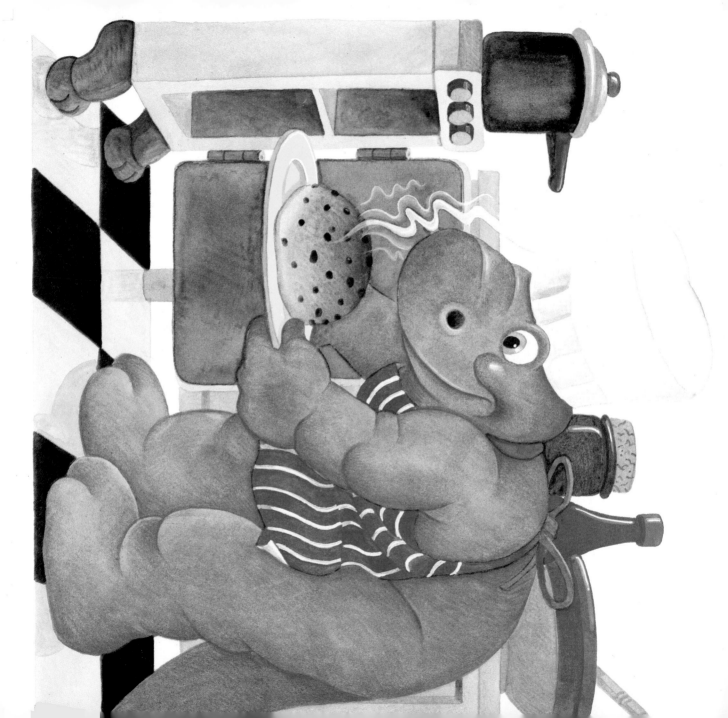

One BROWN dinosaur
baked a yummy treat.

One GREEN dinosaur
picnicked on the lawn…

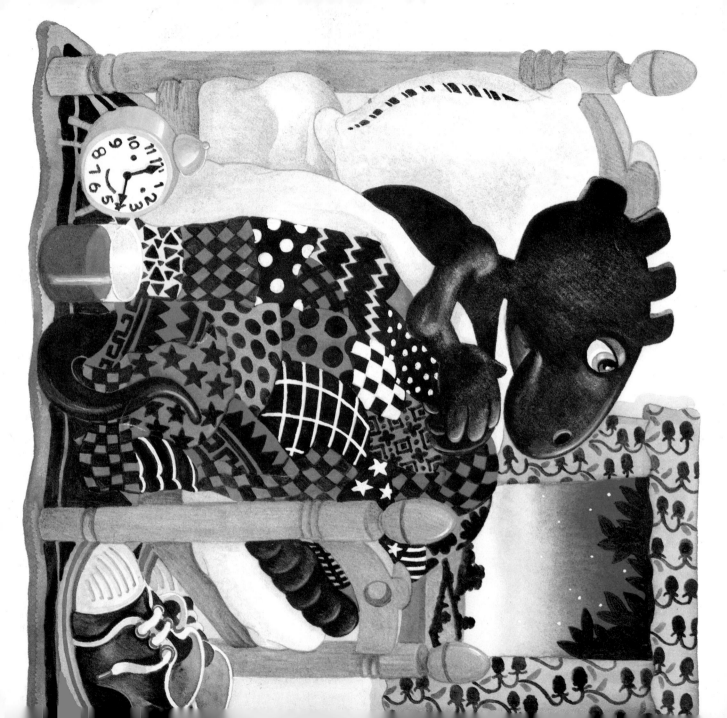

One BLACK dinosaur
waited for the dawn.

One RED dinosaur
made a valentine...

One PURPLE dinosaur
dressed up to dine.

Then all the different dinosaurs
gathered round to play.

And made a special rainbow
to brighten up the day.